I0365413

THE SEARCH

THE
SEARCH

A PLAY BY CHARLOTTE S. AKYEAMPONG

Based on The Pardoner's Tale by Geoffrey Chaucer

© Copyright 2018 by Charlotte S. Akyeampong

All Rights Reserved. Without limiting the rights under the copyright reserved above, this book may not be reproduced, in whole or in part, stored in a retrieval system, or transmitted in any form or by any means (electronic, mechanical, photocopying, recording, or otherwise) except for brief quotations in critical reviews or publications without the prior permission of the publisher or author.

Library of Congress Cataloging-in-Publication Data

The Search, by Akyeampong, Charlotte S.

ISBN: 978-1-7323519-7-4

Includes bibliographical references and index
1. Literature   2. Performing Arts   3. General   I. Title

Editor: E. Obeng-Amoako Edmonds

First Edition

Rights for publishing this work or in non-English languages are administered by Ink City Press, in partnership with Atlantic BG Media.

TABLE OF CONTENTS

Introduction..XIII

Characters..XV

The Prologue   The Tale Teller............................... 1

Act I   Scene I – Endless Struggle 21

    Scene II - Glimmer of Hope.............. 41

Act II   Scene I – Encounter with Death...... 63

    Scene II - In the arms of Love........... 89

Epilogue   The Teller Ends The Tale............... 105

Afterword... 109

Cast/Crew.. 111

DEDICATION

To my parents, Robert and Betsey Newton, and my big sister, Adelaide, who sowed in me the love for reading and writing at a very tender age.

To my husband, Professor Daniel Afedzi Akyeampong—a mathematician, theoretical physicist, lover of literature, avid reader and renowned scholar—words will not aptly describe the joy of a life you made possible for me to experience. You read every play over and again, and irrespective of how many times you saw the performances on stage—and you saw every single one—the pride and cheer in your smile never faded. It gave me the confidence to dream aloud.

To my children Angelo, Adrian and Adeline for their remarkable support. To my grandchildren, whom I am so proud of, for their love.

To my friends, siblings, nieces and nephews, and all well-wishers for their encouragement. To the cast and crew for touching many hearts with their excellent performances of the play.

To my numerous other children, especially my cherished old students of Presec-Legon (*Odadeɛs*) for their loving kindness, and for their positive contributions to their society.

To Kyei Amoako and Obeng-Amoako Edmonds for making it possible for this play to be published.

To God Almighty be all glory and praise for the things He has done in my life.

INTRODUCTION

"To the woods they went, to find, fight and kill Death!"

Ambition drives a heart in search of the realization of a dream, and every stride towards its goal defines and unveils the dreamer's character. When a man, Bolton, dies, three men who had planned to visit him in the hope that he would change their fortunes decide to avenge his death.

In scene after scene, the young men are confident and poised, stunningly delusional and naïve, and they latch onto Casper, their leader's presumed clairvoyant. In a strange way, their logic is honest, as opposed to Pardoner Vincent, whose sanctimonious platitudes leave audiences equally charmed by his wit, and shocked by his tactics. Casper, Jason and Walter throw reason and caution to the wind in pursuit of a wild dream; call it their life's ambition. How far will their firm-minded illusions carry them? What is the worth to them of wisdom and sound advice?

The play "The Search" is filled with ironies that vividly showcase some of the voids in all of our human reasoning, and hilariously exposes the imperfections of the human heart. The central question of the play remains: could it be that in life, whatever we search for, we ultimately find? What happens to the young ladies who live their lives in search of their true love, or to the Old Man whose only hope was to see his grandsons' dreams come true?

"The Search" is an adaptation of Geoffrey Chaucer's "The Pardoner's Tale," and conveys many original cautionary themes to a new audience. Charlotte Akyeampong creates new characters, not only to widen the scope of the story, but also to ensure effective interaction of different characters. For that is the essence of any good drama.

The play seeks to cement the idea that the effort needed to achieve any noble mission is no less daunting than what it takes to achieve a worthless one. The truth is, every one of us is in search of something, even when we don't have the faintest idea what it is we hope to find. Perhaps the flaw in our humanity becomes painfully amusing when it is so glaringly obvious for everyone observing from a distance, but remains one that we ourselves cannot see.

The genuine beauty in Charlotte Akyeampong's "The Search" is how it cleverly uses humour and contrast to arouse the audience's fascination with every one of the characters. In a rather remarkable twist of events, the plot doesn't find a hero. It doesn't search for one either. Rather, the dialogue and music combine perfectly to gently nudge the reader and audience to examine what becomes their own guiding light and ultimately the tuning fork of their lives.

This play was first performed at PRESEC-LEGON, by the Presec Drama Club in 1993. It was also performed many times at the University of Ghana School of Performing Arts (Legon), The Ghana Military Academy (Accra), and in Toledo, Ohio (USA) during a cultural exchange program in 1994 between PRESEC and Toledo EXCEL students.

CHARACTERS:
PARDONER VINCENT – A senior church official
1ST PRIEST — A protegee of Pardoner Vincent
2ND PRIEST — A protegee of Pardoner Vincent
BARMAN — Bar tender at the local tavern
DRUNKARD — An excessive drinker at the local tavern

CASPER — One of three unemployed friends
JASON — One of three unemployed friends
WALTER — One of three unemployed friends
LIZA — Casper's girlfriend
ALEEN — Walter's girlfriend
MANDY — Jason's girlfriend
OLD MAN — Noble elderly man
1ST GRANDSON — Well-mannered grandson of Old Man
2ND GRANDSON — Well-mannered grandson of Old Man
3RD GRANDSON — Well-mannered grandson of Old Man

DEATH
PARISHIONERS — Crowd
CHEMIST

PROLOGUE

THE TALE TELLER

(Background music. A Public House or a Tavern. A barman is busy setting up his place. TWO YOUNG PRIESTS *are seated at a table apparently waiting for somebody.* A DRUNKARD *calls to the barman for his last drink, gulps it down and staggers on, bumping into the* TWO YOUNG PRIESTS.*)*

DRUNKARD

Holy gods of whiskey! Are you blind? Didn't you see me coming? Drunkards!

(Exit DRUNKARD.)

1ST PRIEST

Ogh! Just look at him. What do they gain by soaking themselves heavily in alcohol? But why at all will Pardoner Vincent ask us to meet him in a tavern of all places? I don't get it.

2ND PRIEST

He said he has news for our ears alone. I guess that's why he chose such a deserted place.

1ST PRIEST

Yes, a quiet place, but not a tavern. Couldn't he have chosen a better place? Guess what people will think when they see us, officials of the church, sitting in a bar.

2ND PRIEST

It's true this is a tavern. But it's a very quiet place. It seems not many people patronize it. Just look around, nobody except the two of us, and of course the barman. Perhaps that is why Pardoner Vincent selected it. He wants us to have a peaceful, quiet discussion.

1ST PRIEST

I guess you are right. But why will any man establish his business in such a forsaken place? I wonder how many people do come here in a day.

2ND PRIEST

That should not be our concern. In fact, the fewer we have of these public places the better. And it's all the better if they are sited far away from the easy reach of the youth in particular who easily sell their souls to the devil at such places.

1ST PRIEST

I'm sure those with noses and throats for drinking will find a

PROLOGUE   3

remote tavern by any means. With such people, you know, distance is no hindrance.

2ND PRIEST

You mean people like Pardoner Vincent?

1ST PRIEST

No, God forbid. Why do you mention him? Just as well he's not here to hear you talk of him in this way. Imagine the worthy pardoner sitting among drunkards and gamblers? God forbid, I say.

(Looking at his watch.)

Well, he should be here by now.

2ND PRIEST

You know how busy he is; always engaged in one pastoral duty or another. But he will come. I'm sure of that. Let's wait in patience for him.

1ST PRIEST

Ah, there he comes, and what a crowd at his heels!

(PARDONER VINCENT enters with a crowd following and calling out to him.)

CROWD

Pardoner Vincent! Pardoner Vincent!

(PARDONER VINCENT turns around, facing the crowd.)

4 THE SEARCH

CROWD

Bless us, Pardoner! Bless us, Pardoner! Grant us pardon. Grant
us absolution. Pray for us!

PARDONER VINCENT

In nomine Patris, et Filii et Spiritus Sancti.

CROWD

Amen!

PARDONER VINCENT

Have mercy upon them, Oh Lord, according to your loving
kindness, according to the multitude of your mercies, do away
with their offences. Wash them thoroughly from their iniquities
and cleanse them from their sins. Amen!

CROWD

Amen!

1ST PARISHIONER

I'm going through very difficult moments, Pardoner Vincent.
I'm a farmer and of late, my cattle are dying in their numbers.
Nothing I do can save them. I'm at my wits' end, Pardoner. I'm
ruined! I am down!

2ND PARISHIONER

Me too, Pardoner. There is no peace at my workplace. My boss
is threatening to sack me. Everything I do goes wrong. It's as if
I've been cursed. I pray hard but my prayers are never answered.

PROLOGUE

3RD PARISHIONER

My salary, Pardoner Vincent, it is never enough. I can hardly make ends meet. My wife is always complaining. As for the children, they're forever crying. There is never enough money to do anything. Not enough money for food, for clothes, for rent, and for the numerous bills that keep piling up.

CROWD *(Shouting.)*

Me too, Pardoner. Me too! We are suffering, Pardoner! Things are hard! Life is tough! Life is unbearable!

PARDONER VINCENT

Be patient, brothers! Be patient, everybody. Let's have some quiet, please!

(All are quiet.)

All these hardships you are going through are a necessary part of life. Remember, trials and tribulations are there to test a Christian's faith, to strengthen him and make him a better Christian. Remember, man must not live by bread alone. Therefore anyone who calls himself a true Christian must be prepared to face extreme hardships for the eternal crown. Remember our Lord Jesus Christ himself went through no easy way. Remember the Israelites, forty years did they suffer in the wilderness. May you have patience to endure all hardships. We on our part will continue to pray for you, and fill you with words of hope, wisdom and comfort. Let us pray.

(He begins to chant.)

6   THE SEARCH

"Cleanse them with hyssop and they shall be clean; Wash them thoroughly and they shall be whiter than snow."

CROWD *(Chants)*

"Create in us a clean heart, O God, and renew a right spirit within us. Amen."

1ST PARISHIONER

Thank you, Pardoner. I feel better already. It's as if a heavy burden has been lifted off my shoulders.

2ND PARISHIONER

As usual, Pardoner, your words are a great relief. I'm happy now.

OTHERS

May God bless you! Thank you, Pardoner!

PARDONER VINCENT

I'm glad you feel better. Anytime you have any problem, don't hesitate to call on me for moral uplifting. Remember, that is my duty.

CROWD

We shall do so. Have a good day Pardoner.

(They begin to exit.)

PARDONER VINCENT

Wait! Don't go yet! I have in my bag some holy relics that will help you overcome some of your problems. This bag here contains bones, preserved bones of some blessed saints. If you dip one of these bones into water for your animals to drink, they will never fall ill. Besides, they will multiply very fast. It's only 50 pesewas a bone.

3ᴿᴰ PARISHIONER

Give me one! I'll buy one! That's exactly what I need.
(The TWO PRIESTS assist Vincent with the sale of the relics.)

OTHERS

I'll buy one! I need one! Give me two!

PARDONER VINCENT

This piece of cloth here is from the garment worn by our Lord Jesus Christ before he was nailed on the cross. A worthy moment indeed. This other one is from the Virgin Mary's veil. And whoever possesses any of these shall have inner peace and tranquility. And prosperity will dwell with him forever. They are only 50 pesewas a piece.

CROWD *(shouting for the relics.)*

I want one! I want one!

PARDONER VINCENT

Buy! Buy! Buy! Buy to the glory of God. My relics are the best!
(Very excited, he begins to sing and dance, joined by the CROWD.)

My relics, my relics and I.
My relics, my relics and I.

Oh, what a wonderful treasure,
Gift of God without measure!
We will travel together,
My relics and I.

Your relics, your relics and you.
Your relics, your relics and you.
Oh, what a wonderful treasure,
Gift of God without measure,
You will travel together,
Your relics and you.

My relics, my relics and I.
My relics, my relics and I.
Oh, what a wonderful treasure,
Gift of God without measure,
We will travel together,
My relics and I.

PARDONER VINCENT

And all those who are guilty of an offence so horrible they
cannot confess openly to me here, or those who feel too unclean
to touch any of these holy relics now, can see me later at home.
And by the power vested in me, I will purge them of their sins.
They shall be clean in the name of Jesus.

(crowd responds "Amen!")

They shall be washed in the blood of Jesus Christ.

(crowd responds "Amen!")

PROLOGUE   9

PARDONER VINCENT. They should, however, not forget
their peace offering. They should bring along sufficient money
for sufficient blessings, in God's holy name. Amen!
(crowd responds "Amen!")

PARDONER VINCENT
Go in peace in the name of the Father and of the Son and of
the Holy Spirit. And may the peace of God which passes all
understanding be with you now and forevermore.

CROWD
Amen. Thank you, Pardoner, thank you very much.

PARDONER VINCENT
Have a good day, my friends.
(The crowd leave. PARDONER VINCENT moves to his two
colleagues.)

PARDONER VINCENT *(laughing)*
Ha-ha-ha-ha! Sweet, sweet, simple souls. Oh what a life! Barman,
give me something hot. My throat is dry after all the singing
and talking.
(He gulps down the drink at one go, to the surprise of his friends)

You want a drink too?
(They decline the offer.)

You see, this is one way I make extra income. No one can sur-
vive on the meagre allowance of the church these days. One has

to devise a way of keeping body and soul together, and these tricks have kept me going all these years.

2ND PRIEST

Tricks? What tricks, Brother?

PARDONER

The relics of course. The relics I sell to people.

1ST PRIEST

You mean they are false? They are not holy relics?

2ND PRIEST

You mean you don't sell them genuine relics from the Pope?

PARDONER

I don't have to be accountable to Rome. I therefore create my own relics by simply but carefully picking up bones of pigs and goats I see around. And the pieces of cloth I sell are all bits and pieces of my own old garments, bed sheets, pillow cases and the like. So the money I make is all mine, mine to enjoy! Extra income!

1ST PRIEST

This is forgery. I can't believe this!

2ND PRIEST

This is cheating. It's criminal!

PROLOGUE

1ST PRIEST

Pardoner Vincent, you know this is not right. A man of God should not engage in such scandalous and fraudulent activities.

PARDONER

Calm down, my boy, calm down. Don't work yourself into a frenzy. My relics do exactly what all other relics do, if not better. They provide satisfaction. That is all that matters. Don't worry about the means. The end always justifies the means. So, calm down.

1ST PRIEST

But you must not cheat and deceive the people who put their trust in you. That is wrong!

2ND PRIEST

You must not gain at the expense of others, especially innocent people who have faith in you.

1ST PRIEST

You are not even ashamed or afraid that you may be found out and exposed one day as a fraudulent church official?

PARDONER

Me? Exposed? Here? Never! That will be over my dead body. There is no way I can be exposed. At least, everyone here trusts and respects me. You just saw that yourself. These people believe everything I say or do. May God bless them all. Sweet, sweet, simple souls. They make it so easy for me.

2ND PRIEST

Well, I must say you got me to believe too. When I saw all those relics, I thought they were genuine.

1ST PRIEST

So did I. And to think we even helped you to sell them!

PARDONER

I am not surprised. Nobody doubts me when I speak. Intellectuals as well as simpletons, all fall victims. You know I have a special gift of swaying people with my tongue. And I'm at my best after I've taken in sufficient drink and I mount the pulpit to…

BOTH PRIESTS *(Horrified)*

What? You mean you drink before you preach?

PARDONER

And what is wrong with that? What is wrong with that? I need a wet throat and a morale booster before I preach. Barman, top it up, please. Thank you. You see, a drink soothes the throat, loosens the tongue, makes your words roll off your tongue smoothly and transforms you into a bold, powerful speaker. People simply love you for your eloquence and oratory.

1ST PRIEST

My goodness Pardoner Vincent, you seem to be all in favour of alcohol.

PROLOGUE

2ND PRIEST

Is the worthy Pardoner singing the virtues of alcohol?

PARDONER

No, not at all. I condemn it outright to my congregation. I always preach against drunkenness and other such bad habits, and people are happy, and they offer me money.

1ST PRIEST

Why? Is it because your sermons are morally sound?

PARDONER

Well, I guess so. But more importantly, they're impressed by the way and manner I preach. My style is simply unbeatable.

2ND PRIEST

Whatever their reason is, it's a good service you're doing for the church since the money offered when you preach will be put to good use for the whole community.

PARDONER

Don't get mixed up, my friend, you're talking about the offertory.

BOTH PRIESTS

Yes.

PARDONER

That is different. I am talking about the personal income I make when I preach.

THE SEARCH

BOTH PRIESTS

Personal income?

1ST PRIEST

Do you mean you use the pulpit to generate income for yourself?

PARDONER

Exactly! Why do you think I take so much trouble in displaying the art of preaching in the pulpit? Craning my neck this way and that way, walking up and down, and rolling my eyes in the most charming manner? It's all because of the money I will get. I have to work hard on them, you know. Then with a voice made slightly husky, I spin them a real interesting sermon that knocks them off completely and they give out money for that. You should see me in the pulpit. All my antics are a joy to watch.

1ST PRIEST

This is blasphemy. Such words coming from you? I wouldn't have believed this if somebody had told me.

2ND PRIEST

This is vanity, sheer vanity, Brother Vincent! And what happens?

PARDONER

It is obvious, of course. My efforts are not wasted. One by one, all sorts of people get up and put money in the plate. Every single one for me.

(Sings.)

See them drop their money one by one,
Happily, joyfully they drop them.
Every single coin, whether new or old,
Vincent shall have them all.
He is great, he is good.
He is the very best of preacher we have here.
Every single note, whether big or small,
Vincent shall have them all.

1ST PRIEST

And so that is what matters to you, the money, and not the souls
of the people you are here to serve.

PARDONER

Yes, the money. Do you think I will live in poverty from choice?
Never! That is not the counsel of my inner voice. I will live well
here on earth, and when I die, my soul and all other souls can
go berry picking for all I care.

2ND PRIEST

Oh, no! This is blasphemy.

1ST PRIEST

Such words coming from you, Brother Vincent? I wouldn't have
believed it if someone had told me.

PARDONER

Well, I will tell you more. That is why I invited you here. Barman,
more drink. Sure you boys don't want any? We must be going. I

have an appointment with my lady. She lives in a pretty cottage near Elgin Woods. Come with me, my boys. She's expecting us for lunch.

BOTH PRIESTS

What? You mean you keep a mistress, too?

PARDONER

And what is wrong with that? I too need a friend. Tell me, why do you think Eve was created? You will understand these delicate issues when you grow in this profession.

1ST PRIEST

Pardoner Vincent, you have filled our ears with strange unwholesome things today. No wonder you selected a drinking bar for this meeting. What else do you have to add?

2ND PRIEST

No, we don't want to hear anything more. It's enough!

PARDONER

Just this one. Remember, first and foremost, that I am a man. What's more, that I live in the world and not in heaven, and so are you. You are men who live in this world.

2ND PRIEST

But we belong to the church, and the church is a holy institution of God.

PROLOGUE   17

PARDONER

You are right, my brother. But know that it is only when our worldly needs are satisfied that we can fulfill our spiritual obligations. Nobody can say I ignore my church duties. You just saw how well I'm trusted here. If you boys are as clever as I am, you can enjoy both worlds without any risk. Just know how to play your cards well, that's all!

1ST PRIEST

You are incorrigible, Pardoner Vincent. I give up!

PARDONER

No. Don't give up, my boy. Cheer up. I have taken you boys as my younger brothers. That is why I brought you here to tell you how I manage to keep body and soul together. As you grow up, your private needs and responsibilities grow up with you. I will soon be posted to a new region. When I'm away and you encounter difficulties, think of my words to you. You may adopt one or two of my strategies to keep you going. Or be like the poor old parson and wallow in poverty. The choice is yours.

2ND PRIEST

Well, Pardoner Vincent, I must say you have shocked us greatly with these startling revelations. To think that these things go on in the church! Well, we believe in looking up to God for everything. We'll continue to do so and pray for you.

1ST PRIEST

Yes, Pardoner, we will continue to trust the Lord Jesus to direct us and provide us with all our needs.

BOTH PRIESTS

We are trusting thee, Lord Jesus, for thou alone will show us the way.

PARDONER

Well, time will tell, my boys, time will tell. That's how we all started. Barman, the last one, please!

(Gulps it down.)

Now that I've drunk a good quantity of wine, I am prepared to strike a good story. For though you may consider me a corrupt man, don't forget that I always tell a good moral tale. This is one I often use for my sermon when I'm all out to make money. Let's get going as I tell you the Pardoner's Tale. It is my favourite tale. Once upon a time in Flanders, there lived three good-for-nothing young men; Casper, Walter and Jason. . . .

(As their names are mentioned they come on stage while VINCENT and his friends leave.)

ACT 1, SCENE 1

ENDLESS STRUGGLE

(A tavern; same setting as the Prologue. Enter three good-for-nothing fellows; CASPER, JASON and WALTER. The barman is at post, busy.)

JASON

When, O when will our troubles be over? Each day seems to bring us no luck. We've combed the length and breadth of this town for a job but all our efforts are fruitless.

WALTER

It's incredible. Not even the meanest work is available. Sorrow now follows us wherever we go like a faithful dog, and misery stands ahead of us with open arms to embrace us.

CASPER

We are caught in a web of agony and frustrations from which we find it difficult to extricate ourselves. But surely we shall find a way out. By Jove, we shall. Until then, let's continue to drink our cares away. Barman!

JASON

Yes, let's drink our sorrows away. Barman, bring us something "hot" to start the day with.

(They sing.)

ALL

Give us something hot
That will surely warm us.
Something strong and powerful
That will drown our sorrows,
And make us fit and bold to face the day.

WALTER

Hmm, I just don't get it. We have good education, good certificates, good testimonials, good features, good background, good ideas, good…

CASPER

My friend, stop listing all the good things we have and let's look at what we don't have and see how we can have that too. That's why we are here – to search for a solution to our problems.

WALTER

I'm coming to that! I'm trying to trace the root cause of our problems. There must be something wrong with us. The fault must be with us.

ACT 1, SCENE 1

CASPER

Nonsense. Why must the fault be with us?

JASON

Yes, what is wrong with us, Walter? Just look at us. What fault do you see? Tell us.

WALTER

But why is it that we don't get a job anymore? Why is it that in spite of our many good qualities we are never offered any job when we attend an interview? Why?

CASPER

You want to know why? It is because of nepotism! The top men these days offer jobs only to their relations and friends. If you don't know anybody up there, by Christ's HolyCross, you won't get any work. That's why we are suffering here.

JASON

That's right. All our friends are still down the professional ladder. They are not yet up there to help us down here.

WALTER

Hmm. But I'm still sure there is something wrong with us. We must examine ourselves more critically. We had good jobs once, didn't we? And what happened?

CASPER

Don't ask stupid questions, Walter!

WALTER

Please hear me out. We were more interested in drinking, gambling and wenching at the expense of our work, were we not? Consider the number of times we were thrown out of various jobs, till we became permanently jobless. Do you call that nepotism?

CASPER

That was not nepotism. It was slanderous falsehood. Our enemies told vicious lies about us and got us sacked.

WALTER

Well, whatever. But I do miss the good old days. Oh, when shall I see you again, good old days? How easy it was then to hop from one job to another. If only I had known that this would be my end, I would have clung tightly to one job. Oh, good old days, good old days!

JASON

You keep quiet there, Walter, and don't remind us of the past. Let the past sleep in peace.

CASPER

Look here Walter, we have enough problems on our heads right now to last us the rest of our lives. Please don't set the clock back. Don't set us backward thinking. There is no remedy in that. We must be forward thinking.

ACT 1, SCENE 1   25

WALTER

What can we do now, oh what can we do? *(sings.)*
We are three who are struggling and suffering in life.

JASON *(sings)*

Never been happy since we lost our jobs

CASPER *(sings)*

But we try to be happy with drinking, dicing and dancing

ALL *(sing)*

We do our very best to live.
*(They sing and dance slowly at first, then faster and faster till they
finally sit down, tired.)*

WALTER

Well, I suppose we shall continue to sit here and drink and
remain wretched.

CASPER

Watch it, Walter! We may be poor but we are not wretched.

JASON

No, we are not wretched, Walter!

WALTER

But I fear our hopeless situation is going to send us to our graves
before our time.

CASPER

Jesus Christ, Walter, what is wrong with you? Be positive, man. Why do you mention death? We are not going to die anytime now, no matter what!

JASON

For goodness sake, don't talk about death, it sends cold shivers down my spine. We are too young to die.

WALTER

Say that to Death! You think age is considered when it comes to death? We can all die any time, young or old.

JASON

Stop this talk about death, Walter. I don't like it.

CASPER

Who said we are going to die? We have many exciting moments ahead of us. Mind you, we are yet to get married; at least our girlfriends are waiting for that. And surely Death will not deprive us of the glamour of escorting our brides down the aisle to the altar, with all eyes fixed jealously on us *(he imitates a groom walking his bride to the altar)*. Oh, I'm all for the glamour of a wedding, though I care not a pin for what happens afterwards.

JASON

Job or no job, we shall live to fulfil these happy obligations.

ACT 1, SCENE 1   27

WALTER

Yes, I suppose we shall, with our girlfriends, Liza, Mandy and
Aleen supporting us, I suppose we shall. I'm amazed at their faith-
fulness. They came into our lives when we had nothing to offer,
yet strangely enough they have remained true and loyal to us.

JASON

Not only that. They have tolerated our shortcomings and pro-
vided us with pocket money from time to time, while those who
moved with us when our pockets were full didn't care that much
for us. They loved only our money.

WALTER

Some women are simply nice. I mean, how can anybody fall in
love with wretched creatures like us?

CASPER

Watch it, Walter, how many times do you want us to tell you
that we are not wretched? We are only poor for the time being,
but the tide will surely change. And don't forget, whatever kindness we are getting from these girls now will be paid for later.
I know women. They have a way of reaping back every pesewa
they spend on you.

WALTER

And why not? We owe them a lot, and if they want us to pay
back our debt, what is wrong with that?

JASON

Walter is right. It is by the grace and kindness of our girls that we are sitting here alive and drinking.

CASPER

But do they allow us to drink in peace? Do they? You must not be carried away by their so-called kindness. Look at the other side of the coin too.

WALTER

And what do you mean by that?

CASPER

I mean they are a nuisance, like all women! They are troublesome, always poking their noses into everything we do. They want to know what we are doing and why, where we are going and when we are coming back and who is with us. In fact, they want to know everything. Liza is forever getting on my nerves with her million and one questions.

JASON

Mandy does the same, too. But when I protest, she tells me I should rather be grateful for having a concerned friend around me.

WALTER

I agree with her. We are lucky to have such sweet girls who care for us. See how they search for us when we stay out for long, just to make sure we are not in harm's way.

ACT 1, SCENE 1

CASPER

Are we school boys to be controlled and supervised every minute of the hour? After all, what is wrong with a little drinking, gambling and wenching? Well, I don't want any supervision from any woman, by Jove!

WALTER

Don't be ungrateful, Casper. If we had had this sort of supervision earlier, we wouldn't be where we are now.

CASPER

I told you we are where we are now because of slanderous lies of envious workmates, and not due to lack of supervision. In any case I hate to be supervised by anybody, more so by a woman!

JASON

I won't be surprised if they follow us here to preach to us, "Don't drink, it is not good for your health. Don't gamble; it is bad. The Bible says..."

WALTER

No, not today. They won't find us. This place is very far and unfamiliar. They won't find us.

CASPER

Holy Jesus, we are free today! You must thank me for bringing you to this isolated tavern. At last we can drink in peace without listening to any lecture on morality. Drink and be merry, my brothers, for today, we are free, free, free!

(They sing and dance.)

ALL

Oh we are free to drink in peace, oh we are free today!

JASON

But no, you are wrong, look. There they come with your Liza very much in the lead.

ALL

Oh, no!

GIRLS *(offstage)*

Casper! Jason! Walter!

JASON

There goes our so-called freedom, lost the very moment it was gained.

(Enter the GIRLS who sing and dance with joy on seeing them)

GIRLS

What a relief to see you. Thank God we've found you.

We have been all over,
Searching for you dears.
We've been very worried,
Searching everywhere.
We kept on searching hard, everywhere that we could,

ACT 1, SCENE 1   31

Till we found you here.
Search and you shall find, dears.
That's what the good Book says.
Never give up on life.
Try till you succeed.
We kept on searching hard everywhere that we could,
Till we found you here.

CASPER

What do you want from us? Why are you here? How did you
know we are here?

JASON

We are not kids, girls. We can take good care of ourselves. Why
do you bother to search for us?

ALEEN

We had a tough time looking for you till a friend of yours directed us here!

CASPER *(angry)*

A friend of ours? Which one? It must be Bolton. I'm sure it's
Bolton. Yes, Bolton!

MANDY

No, it's not. Please let's leave this place and go home.

CASPER

It's Bolton all right. Damn Bolton!

LIZA

It doesn't matter who directed us here. The good thing is we have found you. Please stop drinking and let's go home. Drinking is a lecherous thing and drunkenness is a squalor of contention and distress.

CASPER

I told you. There we go with the gospel according to St. Liza!
(The men laugh.)

JASON

Mm.... Bolton. Why has Bolton stopped moving with us? He has not joined us for some time now. What can be his reason for staying away? Could it be he has got a job now?

WALTER

Yes, it is possible. Bolton is probably working. We must look him up tomorrow. Bolton is our man. He will change our fortune. He will help us get jobs.

CASPER

Christ's Holy Nails! Why haven't we thought of that! Bolton is working. I'm sure he is working. We shall see him tomorrow for jobs. He can't refuse us.

JASON

No, he won't refuse us. Holy Mary, this is good news indeed. Our problem is solved! We have found a solution! Nepotism will work for us too. Barman, bring us more bottles!

ACT 1, SCENE 1   33

GIRLS

No, Barman! They will not drink, job or no job.

MEN

And why not?

ALEEN

The drunkard's face is disfigured, his breath is foul, and his embrace is filthy.

MANDY

He totters, lurches and falls like a stuck pig, a disgrace to humanity.

CASPER

The gospel according to St. Mandy!

                                    (The men laugh.)

JASON

Listen, girls, Bolton our friend is a big man now. He is in a responsible position and will give us top jobs. Please allow us to drink to that. We must celebrate our good fortune.

LIZA

No! Drunkenness is the very tomb of human reason and dignity. He that submits to drink can keep no secret and destroys his manhood in the end.

CASPER

Look here girls, for how long will you subject us to this tedious preaching? Please, allow us to drink in peace.

WALTER

Barman, bring the ladies glasses. They must join us in this celebration.

GIRLS

No, Barman! We shall not and they will not drink either.

(Sing.)

Don't sell to them any more strong drink!
We know that will surely ruin them!
For we are struggling and the future is gloomy.
Don't sell them any more we pray.

MEN *(sing.)*

What is so wrong with a little drink?
That you make so much fuss about?
For we are so strong and the drink cannot harm us,
So let him sell us more, we pray.

GIRLS *(sing)*

All is so wrong with that little drink!
We know that will surely ruin you.

MEN *(sing)*

But we are so strong and the drink cannot harm us.
So let him sell us more, we pray.

ACT 1, SCENE 1

GIRLS *(sing)*
Don't sell them any more, we pray.

CASPER
I told you. Women can be very troublesome. They stop your fun, spoil your pleasure, disturb your peace and in fact add to your problems.

LIZA
Don't say that!

MANDY
It's not fair!

ALEEN
We did not come to disturb your peace as you claim. We only came here to remind you of tonight's banquet.

MEN
Banquet? In these rags?

LIZA.
No, *(to CASPER)* I'll get you something very nice which will make you very attractive to all those who set eyes on you.

MANDY *(to JASON)*
I'll also get you most fashionable clothes which will make you so proud and happy to mix and mingle with society.

ALEEN *(to WALTER)*

And I will get you something very modern that will make you very smart. You will walk with your head up, chest out and all will see that you are indeed a man.

MEN *(very excited)*

Ah, you are now talking. We like it when you speak like that.
(A cry of mourners offstage. A funeral hymn is heard.)

ALL

What's that?
(They all move to peep through a window.)

A funeral procession! Somebody is dead! Oh no, not again!

JASON

Why is Death claiming so many lives these days?

WALTER

Barman, do you have any idea whose body is in the coffin passing by?

BARMAN

No, but give me a minute, I can find that out.
(He rushes out and returns soon after.)

Oh no, no. You won't believe it, but it is true. Your friend, your dear friend. Your own good friend is dead.

ACT 1, SCENE 1

ALL

Our friend? Who? What's his name?

BARMAN

Oh too cruel, too cruel. I hear last night, Death sneaked into his room and speared him through his heart, killing him at once. Then he went on his way without a word to anybody.

ALL

This friend of ours who is dead, do you know his name?

BARMAN

Yes, he's your good friend, the same dear friend you want to see tomorrow for a big job.

ALL

Bolton? Bolton dead? Jesus Christ!

CASPER

Oh wicked Death, why should you strike at such a time? Why should you take away our friend Bolton in whose hands our happiness lies? Why, oh why?

JASON

Oh, cruel Death who pounces on the able-bodied youth, and puts a sudden end to their useful existence.

WALTER

Oh merciless Death whose only delight is to cause pain and sorrow, leaving behind tears and misery.

CASPER

At least, cruel Death, you could have waited till we got our jobs from Bolton. Oh, oh, all is lost now.

ALL *(They sing sorrowfully.)*

Bolton, great soul, we shall miss you.
"Great Soul, how quickly thine exodus
To realms of radiant Light.
Go thy way and wait for us
Who struggle in this Life."

(They weep sorrowfully. Funeral dirge in the background)

ACT 1, SCENE 2

GLIMMER OF HOPE

CASPER *(suddenly springing up.)*

My brothers, why are we crying? I ask, why are we sitting here all sad and crying?

ALL *(shocked at his question.)*

Don't you know? Must we repeat it? Bolton our friend is dead!

CASPER

I don't mean that. Why do we waste time crying? Why don't we let Bolton's death ginger us up against Death.

ALL

What? Are you crazy?

CASPER

No, I'm not. Three against one. We can then beat Death mercilessly till he dies. Then Death shall be no more.

JASON

Yah… excellent idea! It's strange nobody has thought about this before. Death has been allowed to take undue liberties with man for far too long.

WALTER

That is precisely the point. Nobody has fought Death before because it cannot be done. The idea is preposterous and impossible!

CASPER

Nonsense! The fact that nobody has done it before does not mean it cannot be done. There is always a first time.

GIRLS

Walter is right. No one can kill Death.

CASPER

Typical woman talk! Look here, girls, we have before us a purely manly matter, a masculine issue, and I don't expect you girls to understand. So please stay out of this. As for you Walter, failure in life has turned you into a nervous wreck and a miserable coward.

WALTER

Holy Jesus! I protest! I am not a coward. I'm only trying to reason like any rational human being. Common sense tells me that we can't fight Death.

ACT 1, SCENE 2

CASPER

And why not? Tell me, do rational human beings consider Death a friend or a foe?

ALL

A foe.

CASPER

Good. Do rational human beings fight friends or foes?

ALL

Foes.

CASPER

So what's your problem? The three of us, three rational human beings, are going to team up against Death, a common enemy, a very dangerous enemy, this very moment and kill him.

WALTER

You don't understand, Casper. It isn't because I don't want to fight, but because Death is a different kind of enemy. We can't fight him the way you are suggesting.

LIZA

Yes, Casper, Death is a special case. He is part of the Divine Order.

MANDY

And no man fights him in the sense you mean.

CASPER

Please stay out of this, girls!

ALEEN

No, we are all involved in this. So you must listen to us. Death is inevitable. It will come when it has to. And we on our part must live pure and straight lives and be prepared to go anytime Death calls.

JASON

But that is not fair. Death should not be allowed the freedom to misbehave in this cruel way, striking when he likes, and killing whom he likes. We must stop him.

CASPER

And we are going to stop him, the three of us, this very moment. By Jove we shall!

GIRLS

Are you really serious? Do you know what you are saying?

CASPER

Sure, we are going to be the three who conquered Death and saved man from the clutches of Death. Oh yes, we shall kill Death and become national heroes.

JASON

International heroes! Since people will travel all over the world to pay us homage. Christ's Precious Blood, we are going to be

ACT 1, SCENE 2   45

famous. Our problems are solved! We are going to be rich and
famous!

WALTER

Well, that sounds good. Perhaps it is worth trying after all.

CASPER

That's better, Walter; you are now speaking like a man. You
see, when we kill Death we shall become great and famous and
people will hail us wherever we go

MEN

"Hail Casper, hail Jason, hail Walter! All hail the three famous
men!"

CASPER

Cheer up, girls, your men are going to say farewell to poverty
and misery, not through nepotism but through our own inge-
nuity and might.

GIRLS

Well, that's better than drinking and gambling!

JASON

All those who laughed at us in our poverty and thought we
were good-for-nothing fellows will be ashamed when they see us
swimming in wealth and fame.

THE SEARCH

GIRLS

We wish you good luck in your endeavour.

CASPER

We shall shun those who will struggle desperately to become our friends when we become rich.

WALTER

We shall live in big, big style,
Move into mansions beautifully designed,
With lovely flowers, fountains and all.

GIRLS

Oh ... that will be great, oh, very great.
We can't wait for that day.

JASON

We shall have servants, many, many servants.
All we'll do is press a button or pick up a bell and give it a shake,
And there they come from every corner,
Smartly dressed servants to do our bidding.

GIRLS

Oh ...that will be great, oh very great.
We can't wait for that day.

CASPER

We shall wear the richest garments,
Studded with diamonds, gold and rubies.

Walk on the softest Persian carpets,
Thickly laid from wall to wall.
Dance to the sweetest music ever,
day and night shall we have fun,
Laughing ever, worried never.

GIRLS

Oh… that will be great, oh, very great.
We can't wait for that day.

CASPER

All right, all right. Now let's hold hands, boys, and let us swear
by God's blessed bones to remain together in this business. Now
say after me.

(Men holding hands,
JASON and WALTER repeat after CASPER phrase by phrase
till CASPER says "fight him", and WALTER out of fear hesitates.
CASPER repeats "fight him" for the two to repeat after him.
Then he continues with the rest of his lines.)

CASPER

We swear by God's blessed bones to remain together as brothers to defend one another as we search for Death, from street
to street, from wood to wood, day and night without rest, till
we find him, fight him and finish him, just as he killed our
friend Bolton and many others. By God's dignity we shall set
off this very moment, so help us God. Amen.

GIRLS

Amen. May things go well with you.

CASPER

Ladies and gentlemen, this is a very crucial moment indeed. Years of pain and agony are about to give way to years of prosperity and happiness. Our life of misery will soon be replaced by one of joy and decency. We don't have much time on our hands. As soldiers of mankind with an important mission ahead of us, we have to get ready for action right now.

JASON

So, Liza, Aleen and Mandy, go home and hold the fort very well in our absence. We may be long, we may not be long. Whatever the case may be, look after yourselves well till we come back to you wearing the Victor's crown of success.

MANDY

We promise to hold the fort very well in your absence.

ALEEN

We promise to remain faithful and loyal to you always.

LIZA

We shall pray for your speedy, safe return.

GIRLS

Until then it's goodbye and go well.

(They sing.)

ACT 1, SCENE 2

49

Go well, brave ones. We pray that you will succeed,
And bring back with you honours that will never fade.

ALL

Long time have we been trying hard.
To end our woes and sorrows.
This day seems to bring brightness back into our dull lives.

MEN

It's time to part. Take good care of your dear selves.
We hate to leave home, but we must win now or never.

ALL

Long time have we been trying hard.
To end our woes and sorrows.
This day seems to bring brightness back into our dull lives.

(Exit the GIRLS.)

CASPER

Well, fellow soldiers, lieutenants of the 1st Class Regiment, we don't have to waste any more time. Our mission is urgent and we shall give it the seriousness and urgency it deserves. We shall therefore move straight into action without any delay. But first, Barman, bring us something hot to warm us up for the task ahead.

JASON

Man, we need the booster now more than ever. Barman, make it snappy!

BARMAN

Yes, sir!

WALTER

That's right, and luckily for us the girls are not here to stop us this time.

CASPER

Fill your glasses, comrades, and let us drink to our success in the impending encounter with Death.
                        (They raise their glasses)

May we meet Death sooner rather than later.

JASON

May we strike him dead once and for all.

WALTER

May there be no resurrection for Death.

ALL

That is to say, may Death die and never rise up again.
            (They empty their glasses by drinking to the last drop)

(Enter a very OLD MAN, apparently looking for somebody.)

ACT 1, SCENE 2   51

OLD MAN

Good day, sirs, sorry to disturb you, sirs. Please, have you seen
three young men about your age and size around this place?

JASON

No, sir, none has been here since we came in

OLD MAN

You see, they are my grandsons. Their father, my son, my only
child, died when they were very young and so did their mother.
And since that time they have been with me. I am all they have
and they are all I have. I must go now and search for them.

(He begins to walk away)

CASPER

Did you notice that?

JASON and WALTER

What?

CASPER

The old man's face, all withered and wrinkled. He is a spy, no
doubt, an agent of Death. Why is he still alive in spite of his old
age? Let's question him. He can tell us something about Death.

JASON

Jesus Christ, you are right. Let's confront him. He might tell us
where to find Death.

WALTER

Holy Cross, how lucky we are to have Death's own agent to direct us to our target.

(They move to the OLD MAN.)

CASPER

Hey, old man, why do you continue to live while younger people are dying? Isn't it time you died?

OLD MAN

My son, I wish I could answer you. I have travelled far and wide, searching for someone to exchange his youth for my old age, but I. . . .

WALTER, JASON and CASPER

What rubbish! Who wants your withered age?

OLD MAN

I got no one, so my age remains my own. I must continue to be so till God in His mercy calls me home.

WALTER

Not even Death will take you away?

OLD MAN

No, Sir, not even Death.

ACT 1, SCENE 2

CASPER *(Excited, pulls his friends aside)*
Did you hear that? I told you he is in league with Death. He works for him; that is why Death has spared him all these years.

OLD MAN
I walk about the earth which is my mother's gate, and knock with my staff from night to noon, crying to mother earth to open her door to me, but she refuses. So I don't know when these bones of mine will be laid to rest. I must continue to live till I'm called away.
(The three men move closer to the OLD MAN.)

CASPER.
You liar! You imposter! You surely know why Death has spared your life all these years.

OLD MAN.
No, I don't.

ALL THREE
Oh, yes, you do! Traitor, liar, imposter, speak the truth!

OLD MAN
Sirs, don't speak so roughly to an old man except when he has offended you. Remember to be polite to your elders and may God be with you. I must go now. My grandsons must be looking for me.

CASPER

By God and the Holy Sacrament, you don't get off so easily!
You are going nowhere until you tell us where this traitor Death
whom you serve so faithfully is hiding.

JASON

Yes, old man you are not going anywhere. We want to meet this
Death who singles out and kills for his delight the fine young fellows around. You are his agent and you go around marking us out
for him to kill! You know where he is so tell us where to find him.

OLD MAN *(perplexed)*

What are you saying? What are you talking about?

WALTER

By St. John, you and Death have teamed up to kill us young
chaps. We won't allow this to continue. You won't go free until
you show us where Death is, you wicked one!

OLD MAN

I have no idea what you are talking about. I don't know where
Death is. I am no spy or agent of Death. Please believe me. I am
a harmless, respectable…

ALL THREE

Stop it, you thieving swine, you scoundrel!

(They push him down.)

Tell us where to find Death!

ACT 1, SCENE 2   55

*(Enter OLD MAN'S THREE GRANDSONS – three respect-
able, well-dressed young men who help him up)*

GRANDSONS

Oh, no! Stop what you are doing. Don't you have any respect
for the elderly?

(OLD MAN sings, assisted by GRANDSONS.)

OLD MAN *(sings)*

You may push a silver-haired man
Down upon the ground, he falls because he's old.
A child never knows what a good man he's got
Until he turns him down, down, down.
So listen my sons, listen to me.
I want you to understand
As the golden sunshine changes into night,
A young man grows into an old man

GRANDSONS *(sing)*

And a man without good manners
Is like a fish without a tail, or a boat without a roller
Or a ship without a sail.
That's a very bad thing in the universe,
A man without manners,
For manners maketh a man.

1ST GRANDSON

Sirs, why do you mishandle a respectable old man like that?
What offence has he committed?

CASPER

Look here young man, don't annoy us with stupid questions.

2ND GRANDSON

The holy Bible says, "They shall rise up before the grey-haired with respect and honour."

3RD GRANDSON

And again, it says, "Do not maltreat an old man when you are young, for another will do the same to you when you are old, if you should live to be an old man."

CASPER

Don't annoy us, I say! Spare us your preaching.

OLD MAN

Thank you, my sons. I'm glad you disapprove of their ungodly behaviour. Hold fast to the teachings of the Holy Book, for he who walks in the light of God shall fear no adversity.

CASPER

By Christ's Holy wounds, drop it Old Man. Don't preach to us. We've had our fill of that kind of talk. Imposter, show us where to find Death.

GRANDSONS

Stop calling him names. You have no right to do that.

ACT 1, SCENE 2

JASON

You are wasting our time. Tell us where to find Death or you will taste the might of our anger.

WALTER

Hurry up! We have on our hands an urgent assignment that cannot bear undue delay.

CASPER, JASON and WALTER

So be quick and show us where to find Death the tyrant!

GRANDSONS (greatly baffled)

Show you where to find Death? Who on earth can do that?

CASPER, JASON and WALTER

Your old man there can do that, so let him tell us quickly.
(They sing.)

Show us where to find him, this tyrant, this tyrant

OLD MAN and GRANDSONS (sing)

It's a request that we can't help.

CASPER, JASON and WALTER (sing)

We've got to find this tyrant!

OLD MAN and GRANDSONS

We've never seen his face before.

CASPER, JASON and WALTER *(sing)*

You know him, you know him.

OLD MAN and GRANDSONS (sing)

It is the truth we are telling you.

CASPER, JASON and WALTER *(sing)*

But you must surely know him, so tell us where to find him.

OLD MAN and GRANDSONS *(sing)*

Oh please, don't force us to do what we cannot do!
*(GRANDSONS go down one before each of the men, pleading
while the OLD MAN goes round them begging.)*

CASPER, JASON and WALTER *(sing)*

You must show us where to find him. We must find him, we
must find the tyrant now.

GRANDSONS *(sing)*

Oh please, don't force us to do what we cannot do!

OLD MAN *(sings)*

We beg you, we beg you!

CASPER, JASON and WALTER *(sing)*

You must show us where to find him.

(pleading repeats over and over.)

ACT 1, SCENE 2

OLD MAN *(speaks)*

All right, gentlemen. If it is your desire to find Death, then listen. Go down the crooked way to the Elgin Woods. I met him there not long ago, resting under a tree. He is not the type to hide for all your bragging and may the good God who redeemed mankind protect you and amend you. Boys, let's leave these reckless ones to their fate.

1ST GRANDSON

You know what? I have this strange feeling.

2ND GRANDSON

You and your feelings. What is it this time?

1ST GRANDSON

I feel that we will come to the end of our search today.

3RD GRANDSON

May it come true!

OTHERS

Amen!

(Exit OLD MAN and GRANDSONS.)

CASPER

Thank you, old man. We shall search for your master Death in the Elgin Woods and kill him when we find him.

JASON

Don't weep when you see him dead, old man.

WALTER

For he has caused too much weeping in this world and there will
be none for him.

CASPER

You see, if we hadn't threatened the old man the way we did he
would not have revealed Death's secret hideout to us. Come on,
let's go to the woods right now to search for Death.

ALL *(singing briskly)*

Let's go to the woods, just now, just now,
To search for Death just now!
We'll fight with him and knock him out,
And Death shall be no more!
And you shall live and we shall live,
And all shall live
Forever and ever!

(They leave. Lights off)

ACT 2, SCENE 1

ENCOUNTER WITH DEATH

(Elgin Woods. Enter CASPER, JASON and WALTER searching for DEATH, looking tired and worn-out.)

CASPER

We are in the Elgin Woods at last, and according to the old man, we shall find Death somewhere here.

JASON

The old man could be lying, for all you know. Perhaps he told us to come this far just to get rid of us.

WALTER

Yes, that is possible. He couldn't betray Death so readily like that. Oh, I'm tired, tired of all this search that may lead to nothing.

CASPER

For goodness sake Walter, don't start it. We have come a long way already. Don't spoil it for us. Our whole future depends on this moment. We shall meet Death any moment from now and we must be in the right fighting spirit to tackle him. Attention! Chest out. Right turn, left turn. Now let's brace ourselves up with the Warriors Special Anthem! One, two!

(They sing):

ALL

Here stand the famous three,
Fearless warriors of our time,
Ready to free all mankind
From the snares of Death!
Marching up and down the woods,
Searching for the Tyrant Death,
We shall give him deadly blows
That will surely finish him.

CASPER

Halt. All right. We shall now take our strategic positions, and spring a surprise on Death as soon as he appears. Jason, go over there and you, Walter, there, behind that tree. Quick, move!

WALTER

Wait a minute, Casper, how can we identify Death? How can we tell it is Death who is approaching since we have never seen him before? We don't want to strike at the wrong man and waste our efforts. Remember, we want to be international heroes and enjoy

ACT 2, SCENE 1   65

fame and popularity and not languish in some God-forsaken prison for killing an innocent man.

CASPER

Yah, you are right. Why haven't I thought about that? But there must be a way out. Wait a minute. Yes, there is a way out. Identifying Death is not a problem after all. It is very simple.

JASON and WALTER

Simple?

CASPER

Yes, easy and simple. Do you remember the old man we saw at the tavern? Do you remember I pointed out to you his face, all wrinkled and withered?

JASON and WALTER

Yes, you did, but what has that got to do with Death?

CASPER

Everything. The two are bound to look alike in every way: height, size, looks and all.

JASON and WALTER

Are you sure?

CASPER

Sure, they are two of a kind, birds of the same feather. All the same, wait till I give you a cue before you strike. All right?

JASON and WALTER

All right.

CASPER

Now take your positions. Left, right, left, right.
(Just when CASPER reaches the tree behind which he is to hide,
he sees a bag of gold and screams.)

Wheew, God's Precious Dignity! Holy angels above!

JASON and WALTER

What is it Casper? Have you seen him? Is he there?

CASPER

What a sight! What an incredible sight!

JASON

Walter, are you there? The cue from Casper. That must be our cue.
Let's move.

JASON and WALTER

Action! Strike!
(They rush to where Casper is, holding their daggers and see the
gold and scream.)

JASON

Goodness Gracious! Holy Martyrs!

ACT 2, SCENE 1   67

WALTER

God's Holy Cross! What an amazing discovery!

CASPER

Is somebody playing a trick on us? Let's look round and see.
(They go round.)

ALL

Nobody. Nobody is here. The gold is ours. The money belongs
to us. It's all ours. By Jove, we are rich! We are so, so rich!
(They sing and dance.)

O what a sight, lovely, lovely sight
That fills our hearts with great joy
And wipes away our tears!
No more shall we go hungry. No!
Never again will suffer. No!
Welcome sweet, easy life,
Which shall be ours forever!

WALTER

What a happy turn of events. By the way, do we still wait and
fight Death?

CASPER

What for? That is no longer necessary. What we have before
us is more than what killing ten thousand Deaths will fetch
us. Besides, this money has put a safe distance between us and
Death. Death is no more a threat to us. Whereas if we dare fight
Death now, anything can happen. I mean anything.

JASON

You mean Death can kill us instead of the other way round?

CASPER

Precisely. You see, Death will be assisted by his agents, and I hear there are thousands of them, and they will use all sorts of dirty tricks to finish us in a most painful manner. I know their type. They are very wicked. You can't trust them. Let's play it safe and leave him alone.

WALTER

Jesus Christ, I am glad we don't have to fight Death any more.

JASON

There is another point, too. Even if we kill Death we may not be recognised as heroes after all.

WALTER

And why not, since we shall parade the streets with the head of Death dripping wet with blood for all to see?

CASPER

Walter, don't be naive. Remember we live in a world where men are ungrateful and very unpredictable. Instead of praising us for the heroes that we are, they may apprehend us for undertaking a job we had not been commissioned for. They may even call us murderers of Death and throw us in jail.

ACT 2, SCENE 1 69

WALTER

Jesus Christ, you are right again, Casper. We can end up in jail.
Why didn't we think about all this before? Oh no, oh, oh!

JASON

No need to moan Walter, we are not in jail, but in the woods
with a heap of treasure that is all ours before us. Look at it and
be comforted.

WALTER

Yah... I am comforted, more than comforted. Who wouldn't be
happy at the sight of such treasure?

CASPER

Well, my brothers, this treasure has been bestowed upon us as
our reward for the able manner in which we faced the unneces-
sary hardships inflicted upon us.

JASON

That is right. We deserve to be pacified. We were made to suffer
too long for no just reason.

CASPER

Providence now wants to make amends so that we don't suffer
again, but live in comfort for the rest of our lives.

WALTER

Wise and just decision!

JASON

Also, I think we are being rewarded for the bold step we took to free man from Death. Not many people will have the nerve to take up arms against Death.

WALTER

Good old God, we are grateful to you for promptly rewarding us.

CASPER

You are smart, God. I like the way you acted fast, as if you know I don't subscribe to an award-giving ceremony in Heaven. I have always said that if there is any good thing for me to enjoy, let me have it right here on earth. And you have done just that. Thank you, God. We shall certainly put this gold to good use.

OTHERS

Sure, we shall.

JASON

You know what? Let's decide what we shall do with our new-found wealth.

WALTER

Right here in the woods? What's the hurry? No, let's go home first, and plan our future together with the girls.

ACT 2, SCENE 1

CASPER

No, leave the girls out of this decision-making process. We shall control our financial affairs ourselves.

WALTER

All right, let's go home now and plan what to do with the money in our secret chambers alone without the girls.

CASPER

No. We can't go home now so long as there is still daylight. We shall be taken for thieves and will be arrested and jailed, or even killed if seen carrying such a huge amount, our own heaven-sent money, through the streets.

WALTER

Jesus Christ of Heaven! O wicked world where everything seems upside down. Imagine the rightful owners being jailed or killed so that some hands that never worked get the money and spend it. God forbid. In that case we shall stay here till dark.

CASPER

How are we going to spend our God-sent money? Let's have some suggestions now.

JASON

I suggest we have our weddings first, then go on a very long mouth-watering honeymoon, visiting all the exciting places we never thought we could see.

WALTER

And after that, where do we take our wives? Do you call our ghettos homes? No, let's buy houses first, fantastic houses, and a fleet of luxury cars and a good quantity of super clothes, and first class musical gadgets and electronic...

CASPER

Hey, hey, Walter, easy, man, easy. The money will not run away. It is all ours to spend. We shall settle all our outstanding debts first and buy everything you have mentioned and even more. It is the weddings that I'm not too keen about. The idea of being tied down to one woman for the rest of my life does not excite me. It's boring. But well, if we must have them, then we shall and they must be grand. I can do with some grandeur, pomp and majesty.

JASON

Sure, we shall have them very big and spectacular. Only the important personalities around will be invited. After all we are rich, aren't we?

WALTER

But this is not fair. What about our own friends Nathan, Josiah and the rest?

CASPER

Walter, Walter, how can you bring in such people? Don't you see we belong to a new class now—high, rich and sophisticated? It will be a come-down to mingle with our former friends.

ACT 2, SCENE 1   73

JASON

Besides, they themselves will not feel at ease in the company of
all the distinguished people we will invite. Imagine Josiah and
Nathan surrounded by a classic display of wealth and luxury.
No, they won't feel at ease. They will be nervous and uncom-
fortable. Let's spare them that agony.

WALTER

Hmm, money can do wonders. It has severed us from our old
friends and pushed us into the front seat with the eminent.

CASPER

Yes, Walter, didn't you know that money controls the affairs of
man? It elevates him who has and surrounds him with an aura
of respectability and dignity.

JASON

And reduces him who has none to a downtrodden, miserable
wretch.

WALTER

All right then, let's invest in some business after we have bought
all our initial needs and paid all our debts so that we don't return
to our former miserable positions ever again.

CASPER

Investment? What for? We shall never return to our former poor
position. This treasure before us has no bottom. It will last till
Doomsday. We shall never be poor again even if we remain
jobless.

JASON

Yah, and we shall remain jobless. After all, why do people get jobs? It is because they need money. But we have all the money we shall ever need in this life, so what's the point in working? To hell with all jobs!

CASPER and WALTER

To hell with all jobs! Let them keep their jobs!

CASPER

Oh, life is going to be exciting. No work, no poverty, no worries. Only fun, fun, fun!

ALL *(laughing)*

Only fun, fun, fun!

CASPER

Can you imagine? From today onwards we are going to walk and talk, dress and dine, live and laugh like rich men because we are RICH!

ALL

Oh yes, we are rich, rich, rich, we are RICH!
(They walk about like rich men, feeling good, laughing loudly and happily.)

WALTER

Oh, this is just too good. The girls should see us. I can't wait to see their faces when we walk in with all this wealth.

ACT 2, SCENE 1

JASON

They will not only be surprised but will be very, very delighted.

CASPER

I'm not sure about that, but one thing I know is they will preach to us. "Too much money is bad. Money is the root of all evil. Take some to the orphanage…"

JASON

You are right again Casper. After preaching to us, they will proceed to question time. "How and where did you get this money? What are you going to do with all this money?"

WALTER

So we must have a story for them. How about this one – that Death was so terrified when he saw us that he gave us this huge amount to keep us away from him?

JASON

A good story! It will not only keep them quiet but will make them respect and admire us, the strong mighty warriors! Mmm, I'm starving. I can't wait any longer. I need to eat before night falls or I will fall with the night.

WALTER

Me too, my stomach is crying for food. What do we do now?

CASPER

I have an idea. Let's draw lots. The one who draws the longest will run to town and buy us food and drinks, while the remaining two look after the money.

JASON and WALTER

Splendid idea!

(Exit CASPER to find three sticks)

WALTER

I can't believe we are rich. Only this morning we were the poorest of the poor. It is all like a dream, a sweet, sweet dream.

(Enter CASPER.)

CASPER

All right, come over and draw. Ah, Walter, lucky man, go to town and buy us excellent food and wine. Remember to walk and talk like a rich man and buy us a meal befitting our new status. Money is no longer a problem.

ALL *(happily)*

We are going to have the very best of meals.
Beef and mutton, fish and cakes
With good wine, white and red.
The same that rich kings will have.
We shall eat and shall drink,
Till we get home late tonight.

ACT 2, SCENE 1 77

WALTER

I will go straight away. My tired legs can perform wonders where money is concerned

(Exit WALTER.)

(Background music as Casper and Jason rest under a tree. After some time, CASPER speaks.)

CASPER

Jason, can you trust me as a brother?

JASON

Of course, Casper. Why do you ask? We have always been like brothers, the three of us, and we trust one another. Why do you ask me such a question?

CASPER

I mean just the two of us. You see, Walter has gone to buy food, and here is a lot of money for the three of us. But if I can shape things in such a way that just the two of us can share all this money, wouldn't you consider that a friendly act? Eh, Jason?

JASON

But how, Casper? Walter knows the money was left with the two of us. What can we tell him when he comes back?

CASPER

Nothing. The plan is simple. We are two and he is one. Two men are twice as powerful as one. When Walter comes back, wrestle with him as if in a game. Then as the two of you are struggling, I will pull my dagger and stab him through his back. You will pull your dagger and do the same. He will die and the money will be ours to share and spend at our own sweet will.

JASON

Hmm. This means we shall lose Walter forever. Poor Walter. He has been a true friend all these years, going and coming with us. Casper, can't you think of another plan that will spare Walter's life?

CASPER

No, there is none. Walter must die.

JASON

Try, Casper, try. I know you are good at coming up with bright ideas.

CASPER

Not this time. I can't think of any other except his death. Jason, think about the huge money you will have. You will be richer and happier and for that better life and greater happiness, Walter must be eliminated.

JASON

Hmm, the power of money! It can make a friend strike at a friend. It destroys with ease, the beautiful relationship that poverty has woven over the years…

ACT 2, SCENE 1

79

CASPER

Be reasonable, Jason! What is so special about Walter? He is but a trouble maker and a coward. He has always been the difficult one among us. You can get better friends to replace him. I can help you find a better replacement, if that is your worry.

JASON

Yah, you are right... I didn't realise at first what you were getting at, but it suddenly struck me that you are right after all... Walter has always been difficult... the way he challenged you when you suggested we team up against Death.

CASPER

That's right. Trust Walter to oppose any bright idea we bring up.

JASON

He also said we were responsible for all our problems.

CASPER

That was a very stupid statement he made. Can you imagine anyone in his right mind digging his own grave?

JASON

He kept on calling us wretched.

CASPER

That is Walter for you, a real negative man who can't think well of his own friends. The lazy fool. I am sure he would have left the two of us to do all the fighting if Death had attacked us. He wouldn't have struck a single blow.

JASON

I think so, too. The moment we got to these woods he complained of tiredness when we had not yet struck a blow. Can you imagine a tired man coming to fight Death?

CASPER

Tired? Holy Mary, he should be grateful to us for doing him this great favour. A tired man needs rest, and he is going to have all the rest he will ever need, now and in the world beyond. We shall make sure of that! Walter, you shall rest forever and ever, eternally. Amen.

JASON

I am surprised we have tolerated his presence all these years. He is damn, slow, stupid, stuck-in-in-the-slime fellow and he must die. I am certain now.

CASPER

And that we shall do for him. Good, Jason. That is the right spirit, man. You are now speaking like a man. I like it when your spirits are high. Keep them high till the deed is done.

JASON

Sure, I will. Now I can do with some rest. The pangs of hunger become sharper and unbearable when one is awake and doing nothing... So let us sleep.

ACT 2, SCENE 1   81

CASPER

Good Idea. We shall kill hunger with sleep and kill Walter after sleeping. Good rest then till he comes.

(They sleep. Enter WALTER.)

WALTER

What, fast asleep on an empty stomach? This would have been impossible a short while ago. But things are different now. The mere sight of the money has lulled them to a peaceful sleep. Money can do wonders. Yes, money is powerful!

(He moves to the gold, and looks at it tenderly. An idea strikes him like a thunder bolt. He moves away from the gold and his sleeping friends)

Lord! If only I could have all this money to myself, I would be the happiest person beneath the throne of God. Holy Jesus, why didn't I think about this earlier? What do I do now? Fight them? No, I can't. I am only one and one cannot fight two. Kill them in their sleep right away? No, it is too risky. They may wake up and catch me in the act. Yes...yes, poison. That's it. Poison has always been reliable and effective from time immemorial. O thank you God... or is it the devil? Never mind. Thank you, whoever you are, for giving me this last minute solution. I have to get some poison right now for the job. I must be off before they wake up. Tired legs, perform your wonders once more, for more money is at stake this time.

(Exit WALTER, running.)

CASPER *(wakes up and looks around)*

I thought I heard a voice like that of Walter. Walter, Walter where are you? Don't play any dirty tricks. Come out now, we are hungry. Don't waste our time. You can't cheat us, you know. We are smarter than you…

JASON *(wakes up)*

Where is he, the scoundrel?
>   *(He rushes onto CASPER and punches him)*

Take this and that.

CASPER

It's me, Jason! Open your eyes. Wake up! Walter is not yet back. I thought he was here, but I was wrong.

JASON

Sorry, Casper. I thought it was him. I guess we are overexcited. Let's go back to sleep.

CASPER

He will come by all means.
>   *(They sleep again. Enter WALTER, followed by a CHEMIST.*
>   *WALTER stops him at a safe distance.)*

CHEMIST

Excuse me Sir, did you say you need the poison for rats or for a polecat?

ACT 2, SCENE 1   83

WALTER

For both! I have a lot of rats I want to kill, and there is a polecat too in my backyard that steals my chickens at night.

CHEMIST

Then the preparation I gave you will do all right. If any living creature eats a mouthful he will die in no time. Yes, he will die within a short time. That is why I ran after you, to warn you that you have in your hand a very potent poison indeed. Be careful where you keep it. Do you still want it or I shall give you a milder one.

WALTER *(Excitedly)*

No, no I will keep it. Don't change it. I prefer this potent one. It will serve my purpose very well. I will get even with any vermin that wants to destroy my life. By Jove, I shall.

CHEMIST

Then you have the right stuff in your hand. It is the best poison in town. But be careful, sir, don't leave it near any human life. As I said, it is highly deadly.

WALTER

That I will not. You can depend on that. Trust me, sir.

CHEMIST

Well. Good day Sir, I am sure you will come back to say how effective the poison was. Till then, good-bye.

(Exit CHEMIST.)

WALTER

Good-bye, Sir, and thank you. Now poison, faithful servant, go in *(he pours it into the food and drink)* and do your work. Since I have eaten already I will just sit back and enjoy the show – the two greedy dogs gorging themselves on the poisoned food and the poisoned drink, then dropping dead and leaving all the money for me. Their bodies can rot here. I will take what matters, the money, and travel to a distant part for a fresh beginning. Poor Aleen, she will wait in vain for me. Oh how she loves me! But I can't go to her without Liza and Mandy asking about Casper and Jason. Well, she can marry someone else. She is a good girl, and I know there are many good men out there who will be too eager to marry her. Oh, life is going to be very exciting for me with all this money at my disposal.

(He goes to his sleeping friends.)

Casper, Jason wake up. I have brought the food. Get up and eat. It's the best food ever!

(They get up and pounce on him and kill him as planned, in spite of his pleas.)

WALTER

Oh, please, don't kill me, don't. . . .

(Walter dies)

CASPER

Well done, Jason. That was a quick, clean job. Now the money is all ours to enjoy.

ACT 2, SCENE 1   85

JASON *(Picks up the bottle and sips the drink as he speaks)*
Where shall we take the money, your place or mine?
(He sips the wine.)

And what shall we tell Aleen about Walter? Oh I feel tired, very
tired all of a sudden. My legs, they are... *(He sips again.)*
giving way under me. My chest... ah... my... chest *(Sips.)* It
is... it is burning... I can't breathe. I think I am dying... *(Sips.)*

CASPER *(going to his aid)*
No, Jason! It is nothing! You are not dying! You will be all right!
All you need is a little rest. Lie down and rest. The attack on
Walter was too vigorous. Fighting on an empty stomach can be
strenuous.
(JASON groans and moans throughout.)

JASON
I am dying... I am dying... My money, my money. Give me
my portion. Be quick... my... mon. . . Casp... Mmm... .my...
Cas...
(JASON dies.)

CASPER
What is the matter with you, Jason? Stop groaning and rest.
What? Jason! Jason! Jason dead? Oh no... Jesus Christ, Jason
too dead! This is impossible. This can't be. What happened?
What an unexpected turn of events! Well, this makes me the
sole owner of this great wealth. Angels above, I can't believe
it. All this for me, Casper? Well if that is the will of God, who
am I to refuse? Now let me take in something first, then I will

see about the money. Which one first, the drink or the food? I am not even hungry. The shock has taken away my appetite. So I will drink first *(he sips from the bottle)* to bring back the appetite. I will take the money *(sips)* and vanish into thin air. No marriage for me *(sips)*– only pretty dames. Liza can go to hell.

(sips)

What is wrong with me? My legs. What was I saying? Oh, I can't see well. My chest is heavy and my head... Am I dying, too? No, impossible. I must live to enjoy my money. Besides I have no intention of dying now or anytime soon. But... but. . . oh my heart, my money, my chest, my great wealth, my gold, O God, don't let me die, please; my. . . my. . . I want. . . to enjoy. . . my. . . mo. . . mo. . .

(He grabs the bag of money and staggers with it till he drops dead).

(Dirge played on flute in the background. Enter DEATH.)

DEATH

O cursed sin, O wickedness! Alas, how come
That man whom God created in his own image,
And redeemed with his precious blood,
Can be so unnatural and wicked within,
And itch to see the face of Death?

Three score and ten has the Creator given man,
But sometimes the Omnipotent, by his own design,
Which man cannot understand,
Calls home a faithful servant before his time,

ACT 2, SCENE 1   87

Or adds more years to his time.
But alas, sometimes too,
Man by his own evil deeds and sinful acts
Provokes Death to come for him.
And so I come without delay,
And cut him down like common grass
For though he gets what he wants,
I get no reward for a good job done.
But I'm never deterred by man's ingratitude.
I will still be around to offer my services,
Swift and prompt, make no mistake.
All you alive, young or old,
Whenever I am invited, no matter the hour,
I will come with joy and take you away
So get it straight, all you alive, so long as you want me
I will keep on coming, so long as I am invited
I will come with joy and take you away.
        (Exit DEATH with the bag of gold. Background music, very
                                                    solemn.)

                        GIRLS *(off stage)*
Casper! Jason! Walter!

ACT 2, SCENE 2

IN THE ARMS OF LOVE

(The Elgin Woods. The GIRLS beautifully dressed for the banquet and searching for the men.)

ALL

Where are they? Boys, where are you? Casper! Jason! Walter!

LIZA *(very agitated)*

We must find them. We are almost late for the banquet. As I said, I have not been at ease since they left. We should have stopped them from this dangerous encounter with Death.

MANDY

But will they listen to us? You know how stubborn and strong-headed they can be.

LIZA

We are going to use force this time. They must abandon this search for Death and come along with us. I have a strong feeling of a coming danger, a premonition. We must stop them.

ALL

Boys, where are you? Casper! Jason! Walter!

ALEEN

Look, there they are.

OTHERS

Where?

ALEEN

There, fast asleep.

ALL

O, thank God! O what a relief!

(They keep their distance.)

MANDY

Poor, poor soldiers! They must be extremely tired. See how soundly they are sleeping even on this hard ground.

ALEEN

So calm and peaceful, with all cares and worries behind them. It is a shame to disturb them.

ACT 2, SCENE 2   91

LIZA

But we must wake them up or we shall be late for the banquet.
We don't have much time.

(They move a little closer.)

ALL

We are sorry to disturb you, boys. Wake up; please we are almost
late for the banquet.

ALEEN

We couldn't help following you here. Come, let us go home. We
have got some elegant clothes for you just as we promised you.

ALL

Wait till you see your beautiful new clothes. Oh you will greatly love them! You'll put them on quickly and we'll run to the
banquet.

MANDY (anxiously)

Have they met and fought Death already?

LIZA

That is not important. We want our men and we have found
them. That is all that matters. Death can go free for all we care.

ALEEN

Yes, our men are dear to us. We must double our efforts from
now on, and change them into virtuous, respectable men. Men
that all will be proud of.

ALL

Sure, we shall. But first, the banquet. Wake up, boys, or we shall be late.

MANDY

You can rest better in your beds. Warm, comfortable beds are waiting for you at home.

ALEEN

As well as delicious meals at the banquet. Get up, it is getting late.

LIZA

It's no use. They are dead asleep. I hear worn-out men can sleep like logs even on the floor. Let's try again. This time with much more force.

(They move very close.)

ALL

Casper! Jason! Walter! Wake up!

ALEEN

Hmm, what kind of sleep is this?

MANDY

Look, a dagger, with blood on it!

OTHERS

Gracious Heavens! What's the meaning of this?

ACT 2, SCENE 2

MANDY

I hope they have not come to any harm.

LIZA *(examining them)*

Oh my goodness! They are dead, all three of them, warm but dead alright. We came too late.

ALL *(In tears)*

O Casper, Jason, Walter, what an unexpected end!

MANDY

You set off to conquer Death but ended up being conquered by Death. Oh cruel, cruel Death!

LIZA

I was not happy from the onset. As if I knew it would come to this. O wicked Death, why should you do this to us?

ALEEN *(sobbing)*

Brave soldiers, farewell. You are at peace now with your maker, where Death cannot touch you.

(Sobbing)

ALL *(singing, weeping and covering the bodies with flowers)*

Farewell, sleep well!
Good-bye Casper, good-bye.
Good-bye Jason, good-bye.
Good-bye Walter, good-bye.
May you be at rest now.

Your journey is over.
Your race here is done.
Doubts and fears are no more.
May you be at rest now.

Farewell Casper, farewell,
Farewell Jason, farewell
Farewell Walter, farewell
Till we meet again.

(Enter OLD MAN and GRANDSONS.)

OLD MAN

My daughters, why are you weeping in the middle of these quiet woods? What is the matter?

1ST GRANDSON

Fair ladies, what fills you with so much grief that you shed such tears that deeply touch our hearts?

2ND GRANDSON

Sweet ladies, don't bear the burden of your grief alone. Let us be partners in your sorrow.

3RD GRANDSON

Trust us, gentle ladies. Speak to us, confide in us and we shall do all we can to turn your tears into smiles, your grief into joy.

GRANDSONS *(sing)*

Speak to us, O gentle ladies.

ACT 2, SCENE 2

We'll do all to end your sorrow.

GIRLS *(sing)*

Your friendly words, O strangers kind,
Your soothing words have touched our hearts.
We shall tell you all that we can

LIZA

Kind gentlemen, before us on the ground lie the bodies of the three young men who were to be our husbands, dead, cold dead.

ALEEN

The life of man, from the womb to the tomb is but a span, a mere bubble. They were up a short while ago, warm and full of life. But now look at them, cold and lifeless they lie before us.

MEN

Oh, no! This is terrible.

MANDY

Alas, poor women! No more shall we hear their familiar voices. Alas poor women, no more will they be part of our daily struggles. They are gone and lost forever.

OLD MAN

Oh what sad, sad news! What a misfortune! How come three strong and healthy men suddenly die like that? Tell us how it all happened?

GIRLS

That, Sir, we cannot tell you, for we do not know how they died.

MEN

That is strange, very strange.

LIZA

But this is what we know, and we shall tell you. They set off this morning, very healthy and hardy.

MANDY and ALEEN

To search for Death and smite him dead!

MEN *(surprised)*

To search for Death and smite him dead?

LIZA

Yes, so they said and off they left.

MANDY and ALEEN

To the woods they went, to find, fight and kill Death!
    (The men move to the dead bodies to have a closer look.)

1ST GRANDSON

Goodness gracious, they are the same ill-mannered ones we met at the tavern this morning who were so rude to us.

GIRLS

They were rude to you this morning?

ACT 2, SCENE 2

2ND GRANDSON

Yes, they showed no respect for our old man here, and mishandled him in a most outrageous way.

3RD GRANDSON

They insisted he was in league with Death and should direct them to the hide out of Death.

GIRLS

Oh how awful! Please forgive them even in death.

ALEEN

I wonder how they met their death.

OLD MAN

I can only guess. My daughters, don't seek to know how they died, for it will be nothing wholesome for your gentle ears. Weep no more, gentle ladies, for men such as these deserve no tears.

1ST GRANDSON

They respected neither God nor man and broke God's rules with impunity.

2ND GRANDSON.

They took the name of Christ in vain with habit- hardened swearing that did them no good.

3ʳᴰ GRANDSON

They did not care for the saying that idle swearing is a sin; neither did they care what happened to their souls.

LIZA

We are not surprised at all, sirs, at what you are saying. We did our best to make them change but they went on swearing and drinking.

ALEEN

We warned them against gambling, telling them it is the mother of all robbery, falsehood, double-dealing, murder, and a waste of time and money. But they paid no heed to us.

MANDY

We wanted them to be virtuous and gentle, but they scolded us and accused us of disturbing their peace with our preaching and morality. But we did not give up. We continued to warn and advise them at the least opportunity.

OLD MAN

But they did not listen, I know. Never mind, my daughters, you played your part well as good Christians should. These men set off to seek Death, not Life, and they have found Death.

1ˢᵀ GRANDSON

Grandfather, did you know they were going to die in these woods when you directed them here?

ACT 2, SCENE 2

OLD MAN

No, my child. I did not have the slightest idea. I only told them what they wanted to hear and what I know would make them leave us in peace. But I'm not surprised they are dead. They were restless and reckless, bent on destroying their lives and souls. They must be happy now, having got what they wanted.

GIRLS

O Casper, Jason, Walter, why did you provoke Death to take you away so untimely?

OLD MAN

Wipe your tears, my good ladies. By your steadfastness and shining example you have proven to be God-fearing and disciplined. You are the type of wives I have been wishing for my grandsons here. They are good souls like you, gentle in manners and hardworking too. They will make good husbands for you. So cheer up, my daughters.

1ST GRANDSON

Grandfather is right. For some time now we have been searching for virtuous, good wives, and the moment we saw you, we knew at once that we have come to the end of our search.

2ND GRANDSON

Our prayers have been answered at last. Our search is over. Gentle ladies, fair ornaments, you shall occupy a special place in our hearts.

3ʀᴅ GRANDSON

We have waited all this time for you, sweet ladies. Take our hands, our hearts, our lives, they are yours.

GRANDSONS *(sing)*

Speak to us, O gentle ladies.
Say you will be ours forever.

GIRLS *(sing)*

Your friendly words, O kindly sirs,
Your soothing words have touched our hearts.
We shall be yours forever more.

LIZA

We came here looking for our husbands-to-be and we have found you. God in his wisdom has replaced the dead with the living, the reckless with the disciplined and has transformed what would have been a disastrous union into one that is bound to be blissful and peaceful.

MANDY

God has wiped away our tears and filled our hearts with joy.

ALEEN

Good Sirs, your gentle ways, your deep concern and kindness rare have won for you our hands, our hearts and our lives.

OLD MAN *(excited)*

Well said, my dears, I am sure Heaven itself is beaming with smiles upon this happy moment, that brings two virtuous parties together. Oh, I am so glad that I lived this long to see this day. So you see, my children, in this world you reap what you sow. Whatever you set out to find, that is what you get. Seek and ye shall find. If you seek trouble you will get trouble. So search for peace and love, beauty and truth, unity and understanding and you will find them all smiling at you. Let the story of Casper, Jason and Walter be a lesson to you all as you travel along life. And may the good Lord bless you and help you to make proper decisions and worthy choices always.

ALL

Thank you Grandfather, we shall abide by your wise words.

OLD MAN *(happy)*

And now come one come all.
Let us rejoice, for God has been gracious unto us.
He has granted each one of us his or her heart's desire.
So why shouldn't we be happy?

(Sings)

Let's all rejoice!
Let's all rejoice!
Let the woodland arches echo.
Let us all rejoice.

ALL *(sing)*

Rise and see this happy union.
Come and join this glorious moment.
Let every heart be filled with the sweetest harmony.
Every voice shall sing the sweetest melody.
Let us all trust in the Lord and search for peace.
Let us all trust in the Lord and search for love.
Let's all serve the Lord God with all our hearts,
And stand straight in His light and do what is right.

(Enter PARDONER VINCENT and his two colleagues. The others freeze.)

EPILOGUE

THE TELLER ENDS
THE TALE

PARDONER VINCENT

And so the three reckless friends, Casper, Jason and Walter, who went in search of Death, met their death. While the old man's grandsons who went searching for love and happiness found exactly what they wanted. Dearly beloved may God forgive us our sins and keep us all from the sin of avarice, greed, drunkenness, gambling, swearing and all that is evil in His sight. And may He make us all worthy of his Holy Kingdom. That, Sirs, is how I preach.

1ST PRIEST

That indeed was a good tale, very captivating and thought-provoking.

2ND PRIEST

Ladies and gentlemen, yours is the moral of this wonderful tale,
the Pardoner's tale, and not the Pardoner who told the tale.

PARDONER VINCENT *(excitedly)*

Don't go please, I'm not done yet.
I have here some great relics all ready and set,
Which I know you'll surely love.
Relics rare, sent from above.
Relics rich, purely divine.
That will ensure your bread and wine.
Open your wallets and bring out your money
For grace and blessings sweeter than honey.
You must be lucky to see me daily,
An honest Pardoner to support you greatly.
Trusted and respected wherever I go,
Selling relics to the rich and the poor,
Relics for the peace you plead.
Relics for all you'll need,
Relics for greater strength,
Relics for better health,
Relics for everyone,
Relics for anyone.
Relics for…

TWO PRIESTS

Enough, Pardoner Vincent, ENOUGH!!

THE END

AFTERWORD

More than 25 years ago, a group of secondary school students in Ghana mounted the stage at their school, PRESEC-LEGON, to portray characters in "The Search," an adaptation of Chaucer's "The Pardoner's Tale." The play highlighted virtues that make a man or woman an honorable member of his or her society. The students were too young to fully appreciate the lessons they portrayed.

We were once the young students, and have through the years become mothers, fathers and active members of the communities we live and work in. The lessons of this play have stayed with us through all these years, and remind us to treat strangers kindly and take responsibility for our own lives. The characters in the play went on their own respective searches; through the years, we've been on our searches, too.

We have learned from the mistakes of some of the characters as well as from the wisdom of others, and our lives are better because of that.

We were honoured to share this story with the world, and we trust that there are more people than we will ever know whose lives have been impacted by this play. From Accra, Ghana to Toledo, Ohio, the message of this play reached audiences. And from the first cold reading to the final curtain call, we were thrilled to share our love of acting with others.

In creating this work, Mrs. Akyeampong shared her talents and allowed ours to flourish. We will forever be indebted to her for the commitment she showed towards her students and to the arts. It is this same commitment that has seen this play become available to readers, both young and old.

It is our sincerest hope that your imagination carries you through your reading of this book, and that you will come along on the journey in a way that transforms your life. That way, the moral of this story will remain with you, even 25 years later.

Our best to you now and always.

The Cast and Crew, 1993

THE CAST

PARDONER VINCENT	Victor Graves-Edu
1ST PRIEST	Ben Odartey Tawiah
	Nathaniel Aguda
2ND PRIEST	Fred Kwawuvi
	Seth Asante
BARMAN	Ken Okyere
DRUNKARD	Ben Asomaning
CASPER	Kyei Amoako
JASON	Nii Otu Okonnor
WALTER	Michael Commey
LIZA	Nadia Sam
	Naa Dede Oboshie Badger
ALEEN	Irene Jemilla Mahama
MANDY	Angela Anarfi
OLD MAN	William Adjei
1ST GRANDSON	William Ampadu
2ND GRANDSON	Ekow Mensah
3RD GRANDSON	Kwame Agyarkwa
DEATH	Joseph Anim Addo
	Reginald Atta Kesson
	Alhaji Sanhoon Amin
PARISHIONERS	Kofi Glover
	Kodjo Koram
	Kwamena Gilbert-Arthur
	Alfred Saforo
	Socrates Olympio
	Colin Akoto
	Jerry Insaidoo
CHEMIST	Ben Asomaning

THE CREW

DIRECTOR	Ababio Gyebi
ASSISTANT DIRECTOR	Kwaku Duah Berchie
ASSISTANT DIRECTOR	Eric Ansah Brew
CHOREOGRAPHER	Terry Bright Ofosu
ORGANIST	Yaw Acheampong Pare
ASSISTANT ORGANIST	Kwesi Dei Awuku

PROPS

Tavern furnishings:

- Bar
- Tables and chairs
- Drinking glasses

"Relics" - A tote bag and pieces of cloth and bones

Stuffed sack of gold pieces

Two daggers

Vial of "poison"

Bag of food and wine for WALTER

Flowers

www.ingramcontent.com/pod-product-compliance
Lightning Source LLC
Chambersburg PA
CBHW060456080526
44584CB00015B/1452